GREGORY A. BOOKER

INSPIRED WRITINGS
OF A
PROPHET
FOR
JESUS
THE
CHRIST

INSPIRED WRITINGS OF A PROPHET FOR JESUS THE CHRIST

PROMINENT
BOOKS
EDGE

5830 E 2nd St, Ste 7000 #9983
Casper, WY 82609
USA

CONTENTS

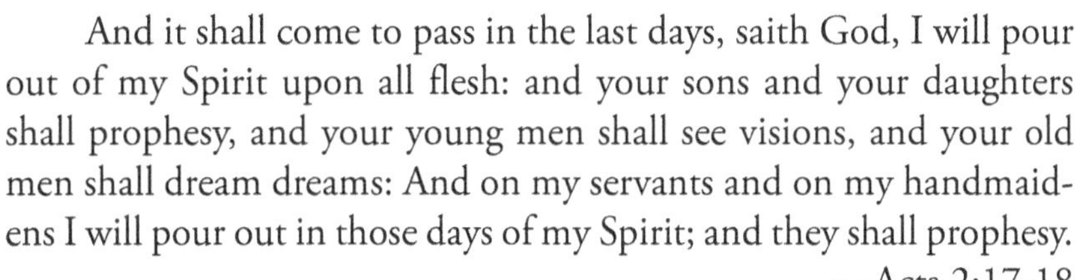

And it shall come to pass in the last days, saith God, I will pour out of my Spirit upon all flesh: and your sons and your daughters shall prophesy, and your young men shall see visions, and your old men shall dream dreams: And on my servants and on my handmaidens I will pour out in those days of my Spirit; and they shall prophesy.

—Acts 2:17-18

PREFACE

A Statement of Vision:
The Upper Room Visit

ON A COLD winter night in Rockford, Illinois, a group of writers/poets sat around a table reading their various works. The purpose of the meeting was to share our talents and, more importantly, to express our faith in our Lord Jesus. On this particular night, the thought of what this could lead to entered my mind. Here we were down in the lower level of the public library. However, I sensed the Lord was making it His Upper Room. All of us were coming from diverse backgrounds and covering all ages and denominations. We were few in number, but new faces continue to show up at the meetings, giving us new insights and always the joys of a believer in Christ. Clearly something was going on as the Lord continued to draw others to this creative venue in our hopes of publishing material with Jesus as our focus.

Reflecting on the crucifixion of Christ, by the time Jesus breathed his last breath on the cross, there were only two men willing to openly take Him down from the cross. They were Joseph and Nicodemus, for the disciples abandoned the cross out of fear for themselves, but God always has someone to do His work. So it didn't matter that the disciples were not present. For by the grace of God, Jesus held nothing against them. Jesus showed them a resurrected

Savior, and they continued to be His disciples, and their hope was restored.

During Jesus's post ministry after His resurrection, what was twelve disciples became 120, waiting for something of which they knew not of. They were directed to wait and to wait together in the Upper Room, expecting. Then on the Day of Pentecost, their faith was rewarded and empowered; they gave birth to the Church, and the world hasn't been the same since. I believe that such a phenomenon is being established now in these perilous times by the Spirit of God. A quest for the righteousness of God in a self-righteous world. The world is in a deep pain as it struggles to live with a God but with disregard for any truths or laws from God. Such was the case, and in the Upper Room, those 120 precious believers were being set to restore God's position. They were moved by the Spirit to preach Hope through salvation, and the platform was Christ and Christ only. After the passing of approximately two thousand years, could the world be falling back to those times and in need of the reality of God through divine intervention once again on an even a grander scale, if you will?

The Rockford Christian Writer's Guild had a vision to put their faith in Lord Jesus in print. It's an effort to express, share, and promote through the pen *how* the Lord continues to work through those who He touches with His Spirit. I personally have found more joy *being* in the Lord than *doing* something for Him and, as result, seem to do even more for Jesus. Such is the essence of the collective works of inspired writings that make up this book. In this presentation, you will find poetry to prophetic utterances, even psalms. It would be easy to let them collect dust on a closet shelf, written but never read. Thoughts that are never spoken! This position I chose not to take, hoping just one unbeliever may be touched to know the Word is our Light and in it, nothing is hid.

And what is the purpose of these writings? Personally, I want to *restore* the faith and the hope that was set two thousand years ago, with prophecy being the vehicle of delivery as the Spirit giveth. Let us remember that Jesus is the spirit of prophecy, and He is The Prophet of prophets. I simply work in His office. These inspired writings are meant to speak His hope and His forewarning in preparation of a deliverance to come... someday. I just pray daily that I put forth the prophetic word, being also a part of His ministry, for the glory of God and bringing others to that marvelous light. In 2 Peter 1:19-21 it is written: "We have also a more sure word of prophecy. where unto ye do well that ye take heed, as unto a light that shineth in a dark place, until the day dawn. and the day star arise in your hearts. Knowing this first that no prophecy of the scriptures of any private interpretation. For the prophecy came not in old time by the will of man: but holy men of God spake as they were moved by the Holy Ghost."

In my study of God's Word, there is a consistent error that is made by the people of God throughout biblical history. We fail to ask God what is His plan for Himself? Being too concerned with ourselves, all too often, this is the higher purpose that we never seem ready to hear. I have searched the scripture diligently for His purpose for Himself and have been inspired to write the experience for the benefit of the Church. Let's meet once again in the study room of our mind in preparation of His Return because I got the feeling that the Lord is making ready a fresh anointing for the New Millennium. Peace be unto you through our Lord the Christ.

"AND THE HAND OF THE LORD WAS UPON ME"

(A BAPTISM BY THE SPIRIT)

IT HAPPENED ON a day in April of 1990, in the living room of my home being alone… very alone. I had left work early just to study the Bible and pray. Seeking for something that I knew was there. I continued to attain a higher understanding of Jesus Christ. Sitting on the sofa and reading a book titled *Sermon on the Mount*, I suddenly laid my head back, meditating on His Words and ultimately His Righteousness. Without realizing it, I began to slip into a trance… a very deep trance. I found myself unable to move but being moved nonetheless, for there was a weight upon me that was driving me slowly but surely from the sofa to the floor. I was laid prostrate, and the weight continued to press upon my back. Attempting to get up, I could not do so literally or in the vision. Yes, there was a vision set before me. For as I struggled to get up but could not, at the tilt of my head, I saw a stake set in the rocky ground. It was like dusk, and all I could see was the base of this stake for there was nothing else to see.

Suddenly, I had an eerie and yet profound feeling that *someone* was hanging on that stake, and that someone was me. I remember thinking, *Why am I thinking of me hanging on a stake if I am laid upon the ground?* Yet this is what was puzzling me throughout the whole vision. I therefore struggled to gaze at the top by slowly and with much effort traveling up the stake with my eyes for there continued to be a weight pressing firmly on me. Attempting to stand, I could not! As I raised my head and eyes, I came upon the feet and then the knees. It was dusk, but I was determined to see the waist, then the torso. I truly felt that I would see myself hanging on the cross. I felt dead and yet I was alive.

Certainly I was anticipating myself to be hanging on that stake for I also felt my sins. Yes, the weight of my own sins seemed to condemn me for I knew I was before the Lord. I saw the shoulders, and then I saw the head. Falling forward, the whole body literally was torn and bleeding. I gazed in amazement. Yes, even awe, if you will, and yet I felt utter shame and ultimately fear, but oh, was there also so much joy. For it was not me who was on that cross. It was someone else! I whispered, "Is that Jesus?" I knew He had taken my place for it was I who should have been up there, and yet there He was through no fault of His own.

Suddenly, a Voice boomed out of the sky, and then I found myself standing on my feet, and the Voice said most profoundly, "THIS IS WHAT MY BELOVED SON HAS DONE FOR YOU." I cried as I fell to my knees, thanking my Lord indeed. The Voice was fearful, but now it was not given unto me to fear for I felt whole, even renewed. I felt baptized by the Spirit of the Lord. The Vision was then ended, and I opened my eyes, finding myself on the floor instead of the sofa where I had sat. I was sweating and had lost all concept of time. Though it seemed short due to the events. I did know that it was not, for the clock approximated over an hour at least.

I asked myself, *Did I have an out-of-the-body experience?* This I may never know, but this I do know: "I am crucified. Nevertheless, Christ is alive in me." I did thank the Lord for His long-suffering patience toward me and acknowledged before Him that I am at His service. I continued to study the Prophetic Word of the Lord, and on May 16, 1990, while at work in my private office, a Voice came upon me and said, "Now write what you have come to know." Without hesitation, I wrote my first Prophetic Letter, and so began a work that the Lord has called me to do. And this is the Work:

"The Necessity of the Return of God's Chosen People"

SEVEN LETTERS DETAILING
THE PROPHETIC FRAMEWORK OF
THE RETURN OF CHRIST

"AND THEY WALK WITH THEIR HEADS DOWN"

(A VISION OF THE CROSS)

SO THERE WE go, all of us walking through life. Feet slowed with our step being guided, but not knowing where. Heads down… All heads are down. Millions upon millions, walking a slow but steady pace. For some unknown reason, many are afraid to look up, but they do look at something if only to walk around it, lest they bump into the obstacle. The walk of mankind is the fear in Adam. "I heard the voice of the Lord in the garden, and I was afraid because I was naked, and so I hid myself." And the Lord said, "Who told thee thou was naked?" Adam never did answer the question of who told him he was naked. He seemed too anxious to place blame when what was needed was admitting fault! Yes, this is the walk of Mankind. In the garden, the obstacle was the voice of the Lord, but on Calvary's Hill, the obstacle is none other than the Cross. And all mankind travels the path of life with this obstacle in their way. This is my vision at the cross.

Mankind travels the path that leads ultimately to Calvary's Hill. It is God who has predestinated Man to walk this path, but it is Man who decides if he shall travel it, looking up or looking at the cross or not even looking at all. I walked such a walk, but now a vision is given unto me. The Cross is at the top of the hill, unmovable by time, and none can remove it though they may try. So heads are down and their souls are hid as they walk the path that is laid down before them. Each man senses that something is in the path of his way. Most will simply follow the path that others beside them walk. Seeking not to question, they receive no answers.

As they approach the cross, most walk around it without even looking up, let alone looking at. As they merge back together after being split by the presence of the Cross in the middle of the hill, they do look back to see what caused them to split. And when they do look up at the back of the cross, they see no one! Thinking themselves the wiser, they walk in their pride, unashamed of their sins. Since they see no Christ on the cross, they see no need for salvation. It is the time they choose to look up that blinds them. This is Religion!

And then there are those who look at the Cross, failing to look up at the Christ. They see the stake in the road and lean against it to rest. They find that the stake is comforting, and they raise their hands, assimilating the posture of the One above them. Hence they become a fair distraction as multitudes upon multitudes pass by. They do attract a great many who stop to soothe their bowed heads that they might not hide with closed eyes. They admit that Someone is nailed to the cross. "Better Him than me," they say. Being at the base of the cross, they have no need to pick up their cross and deny themselves for they are too busy attracting others to its base. No need to climb up when we can just stay down! The Spirit acknowledges these as the institution of Christianity. They have the knowledge of the word but do not give their heart to the Christ.

And then there are those who, as they walk in the crowd, as they stand at the base of the cross, for some unknown reason, look up, gazing in amazement at the bloodied disfigured man nailed to the Cross. They search the Cross for all its purpose, but more significantly is that they react to its Error, for He was found without Sin in His Body and undeserving of the death Man placed upon Him. Thus we are found guilty of what we already were… sinners! These, they hide no more from the Voice the cross represents. They fall to their knees, recognizing that they should be nailed to the cross, and therein is found the grace of God and so they repent!

The Spirit of the Cross then lifts me up and sets me out of the multitudes on the sideline. Eyes are opened and my head is straight, and I am told to beckon to the crowd to "Look up… Look up!" But only so few do as we walk with our heads down. For to carry your cross, you must be willing to be placed upon it! This is the victory, and this is the vision I was made to see, and these on the sidelines are the sealed!

THE PASTOR AND THE PROPHET

These are the words the Lord has spoken:
For our determination has been found before His Throne
And He has heard the desires of our hearts.
And so a place shall be established… yea
A habitation that the Spirit of Him might dwell
In the fullness of His Truth.
And in My House shall tears be brought before My Altar.
That there should be joy and joy unspeakable.
For who can know me lest my righteous judgment touch thee.
So let the minister lead and shall the prophet proclaim.
Let the minister protect and the prophet advise.
And shall my minister build the walls
But my prophet shall be without blueprint. For he is mine!
Let these things be. Lest the congregation be overwhelmed
And My Word becomes hindered.
Therefore, I sanction thee to work well in My House.
For the work of the ministry is for
The perfecting of the saints
That they might know the fullness of Him whom I have sent.
Therefore, bring me the fruit of their repentance.
That my Spirit might settle upon the weak
And the lame, the hurt and the fearful.
Yea, even the poor and the lost who need to be found.
I counsel thee to Stand at the Door of My Gate and
Sound the Trumpet of Departure that they might taste
That which is Hope and Hear that which is Pure.
Sound it well that my Spirit might hear thine expectation!
And know for a certainty thy precious Faith.
That it is in my Son, the Christ, the Blessed Redeemer.
Hold fast to that which is true, my Church.
For the God of Israel is set to speak once again.
And it is His righteousness, which shall be declared by his prophets.
So gather the flock my ministers!
That we shall make way for the Lord of Lords and King of Kings.

Savior to the Gentiles and Messiah to the Jews. Amen!

To the Churches, let us place these words in the center of our hearts
that they might be found at the entrance of His Church.

GREETINGS, MINISTERS OF THE CHURCHES AND THE CONGREGATION

THE WORD IS declared, and the moment has been established. For this is the "times of restitution" bringing forth the coming of our Lord and Savior the Christ. For if the apostles can declare it, then why, with all we are made to see, cannot we declare it now! By the grace of God, there is one who works in the "office of a prophet" in the House of the Lord. The Lord has found him, one who is determined to speak the prophetic word of God. For I am commanded to publish these words before the congregation that they might know, and I pray they may have belief in the ways of the Lord. For it is written, "My people perish for lack of knowledge" and "Where no counsel is, the people fall, but in the multitude of counselors there is safety." I am but a counselor and a messenger in the name of Jesus.

The following articles are four statements of "prophetic utterance" to the church and for the church but not necessarily by the church but by the Spirit. I appeal to one and to all to consider these words that they might be profitable to your ministry. The following is a short synopsis of each:

A. The first, "The Declaration of the Mystery of the Last Days," reveals the mystery of God unfolding in end times as the scripture states. It announces to the Church to prepare for final deliverance from judgment. In addition, it issues a warning to an unbelieving world concerning his prophetic word on the Jews' return as a nation, thereby proving the reality of his word on earth. Finally, it also declares to Israel a deliverance to come despite their unbelief in Jesus as we see now. God is going to show to the world that His love will be the greater? He will deliver Israel at last and yet judge a world that rejects His grace.

B. The second and third letter of utterance speaks specifically to America, God's country as we have declared. It has become a place full of disobedience to the laws of God, and even the churches do seek to justify their own sins. Bringing to life the words of the apostle Paul, which read, "Let no man deceive thee. For the day of the Lord shall not come, except there come a falling away first. Then that man of sin shall be revealed. The son of perdiction" (2 Thessalonians. 2:3). Five of the the seven letters addressed to the churches in the Book of Revelations chapters two through four reveals a sad conclusion. Jesus admires their works but declares they have forgotten their first love… Him. He request of them to repent. Clearly in America, our churches consisting of it's many denominations and cultures are failing to sustain pure and sound biblical doctrine. With true repentance before our God being practically nonexistent among much of the christian's community. Many members come to church but fail to come to Christ and as the institution of Christianity weakens so shall America the nation.

C. The fourth letter is a word concerning God's righteous judgment. In essence, would it be fair to try only Israel by Christ's first coming and not also try every other nation by his second coming? As Christ tested Israel, the Holy Spirit has made me to see how God is using Israel to test the world to see if the gentiles believe the word concerning Israel's return as Israel was required to believe the prophetic word concerning who Jesus Christ was. I declare that our religiosity is doing the same thing to us as it did to Israel. The question I ask is, could we reject within our hearts the reality of Israel's salvation fulfilling scripture at last? Would not this act restore and prove absolute truth to the glory of God and no one else? Could God be showing the world ***what truth is and where it sits! That it's inside the gates of Jerusalem when the battle rages in the Valley of Jehoshaphat which is on the other side of that gate?***

We the church ought to be saying what a mighty God we serve as this reality nears with each passing day? God word warns us in

Romans Chapter 11 not to be boastful, envious or jealous in that day but to prepare to see righteousness about to be performed when Zion the Deliverer comes! This letter addresses these concerns because I see so many sleeping saints in the churches across America and the time is short. For when the preacher of righteousness speaks, he is usually called directly by God to declare it and I sense it to be the final call even the last resort.

Do come that we may have eyes that we may see and ears that we may hear. That a rejoicing may begin within our hearts, and the promotion of the Gospel might reach out to a lost world one more time. For the Spirit of Truth shall declare his story through the prophets of the Lord in the hour that God himself determines it. And let our hearts know it is only fair that if first the Jew, it is now the Gentile test and this is the Lord's righteousness that He is set to perform! I hope the following four letters of prophetic utterance add knowledge and wisdom giving the church clarity all of which belongs to the glory of God. I am but a cry in the wilderness!

Purpose: For the Perfecting of the Saints

Ephesians 4:11-13, "utterance in the year of 1995"

THE DECLARATION OF THE MYSTERY OF THE LAST DAYS

The Lord God whom we serve… is a living God
Full of grace and tender mercies
Oh, but is His anger to be kindled
And His heart to take offense in that great and notable Day!
Let us hear His justice that we might know our sins.
Has not His Son been falsely accused?
Oh, do man quest for that which is right… all men!
Yet he sees not the injustice against one found even without sin.
For the Lord has published it before all the peoples of the earth.
But their ears are plugged and eyes are shut.
Righteousness to them is only for them indeed.

How foolish is thee who questions not!
That no answer can I give when no question is asked.
Thou runneth from me, oh man, running into mine adversary.
For remember, there is an enemy in the path.
And his time draweth near and his kingdom is fallen.
And so shall the kingdoms of yours, oh man, do likewise.
Shall you not be full of anger… full of desperate lies when I, even I,
     the Lord, say enough!
Thou shalt know it most assuredly.
By the mouth of my own prophets shall thou know it.
Rise up, my Church, and hear them well.
For I have come unto you to speak as I have to my own nation.
The earth is thine wilderness
And the New Jerusalem shall come down upon it.
So shall my prophets prophesy concerning Jerusalem.
For it is full of strife, full of division, and is now
The blood beginning to flow as I knew it would.
For there are giants in the land, my Church
But do remember the report of Joshua and Caleb.
For they believed by faith and was rewarded and so must you!
Oh, my prophets, do look upon Israel the nation lest
I send prophets from Israel the nation.
Church, do consider this ancient nation in these modern times.
For it is my written word moving before all the earth.
Has it not been spoken from days long gone.
And yet I am refused! But I AM THAT I AM… as then
And with a great thunder, I AM THAT I AM… even now!
My people are few in the midst of many.
Is it not for a demonstration?
Remember by my ancient prophets did I not speak
That I do this not for their sake but for my namesake!
For my nation is full of pride and indeed boastful.
But what of you, Brazil, and what of you, Iran and Italy and
China and Russia and Nigeria and oh, so many other nations.
I ask do you serve me… Do you declare my Son?
And do I have tears for my America… tears indeed!

You have refused to hear my trumpets as Israel refused in the wilderness.
Come ye out of her, my saints… for she is fallen! She is fallen!
Therefore, publish this before the congregation,
That they might know, oh man.
For to know me is to hear me… Such is My righteousness.
So hear this and hear this well… for the words are a certainty.
Ask the Lord again the question, "Will thou at this time restore again
    the kingdom to Israel?" as it is written.
Ask indeed, my Israel. That I might provide the answer!
For thus saith the Lord concerning the question.
This is how I shall put all things under the feet of my Son.
I shall permit a weight to come upon the backs of Israel
And they shall be heavy laden with burdens.
And you, oh Gentiles, shall perform it so!
You shall serve me well in your unbelief concerning My Word
And Israel shall cry out when all the world is encamped around thee.
When their politics, their armor, their economies, and even their gods
Shall seek to bring my nation to its end.
Shall then my nation say, "Come, my Lord, do Come!"
Can they repent? Will I yet cast away their transgression against me?
Does not my Word declare that salvation shall rest in Me? So shall
    it be!
For there will be no other nation, people, weapon, or hope
That can save thee but by Him that was rejected.
Is it not written by my prophet Zechariah
"Then shall the Lord go forth, and fight against those nations,
As when he fought in the day of battle. And His feet shall stand in that
Day upon the Mount of Olives, which is before Jerusalem."
I ask what other god can declare such a purpose?
And make known such a mystery that is before all the earth!
How precious is the work of mine own Son… Savior to the Gentiles.
And shall I also demonstrate… Messiah to the Jews!
I declare to all those who have an ear, it is not the Church or Israel
But the Church and Israel! And by my Son shall they both be one
    new man.
And then the scripture shall be fulfilled as written in Romans 11:15

"For if the casting away of them be the reconciling of the world, what
        shall the receiving of them be but, life from the dead."
And therein shall the Lord God be glorified
And all the earth shall see it and know it.
Oh indeed, How sweet the grace of God.
Who can measure His grace and who can perform His mercy!
Beware, Gentiles. Prepare my Church for that great and notable day
        is now.
Behold, I will make all things new in that hour as promised to those
        who believe.
For the Earnest Expectation is indeed the Blessed Hope.
Look up, the Lord declares, I say look up for the visitation!
Thus have the Lord written. So shall my prophets declare it!
Let us hear a prophet's cry for his country. Written in July 1991.

TEARS FOR AMERICA

Oh Land… Far from the Apple of my Eye
Great has been thy calling… A place of refuge for the many.
Some out of necessity and some by the yoke.
Yet has not all been blessed in its Promise?
Did not we put our Hope in thee… the Lord!
Despite the error of our ways, we stood corrected
And blessed in His knowledge none the same.
Many indeed, yes, many a seed among men.
Having the same dreams… the same hope… and the same God.
Blessed were we as the Lord smiled upon us as we sought Him out.
But oh, America… Where are thee now? Cannot the Lord ask?
And can we answer the question while we are caught up in the
Fruits provided and hearing not His Voice?
Do the children know His ways for to tell their own? I think not!
Mighty America, everyone in you cries for things to be their way.
There is no contentment, and where is the unity?
They cry not for the Lord anymore for they know Him not!
Oh, America… an arm of support to my chosen, are you compromising

In your success? In the name of democracy you gained freedom.
But was not your freedom founded on Truth!
Therefore, are you not being swallowed up in your own design?
Yes… diversity being your promise can also become your curse!
Where is the truth when you honor
The lies of those afar in your politeness?
Oh, America… Have you not abandoned your own children
Preferring to court the favors of outsiders for the few inside?
How long, land of the free? How long, land of the free?
We are burdened by our greed… Enslaved by debt of our choosing!
With our God we are neither hot nor cold but lukewarm…
Giving in without giving our all, only to give up!
Therefore, I have Tears for my America.
Yes… the hope of the world has been in thee.
And I can see none finer in the Lord than America.
Therefore, I have Tears for the World also.
For when America speaks no more for the True God…
Then the True God must speak for Himself,
And then there shall be tears in America… Tears indeed!
Thus the Lord do Saith… Amen and Amen.

And it is written concerning he who prophesies: "And if thou say in thine heart, How shall we know the word which the Lord hath not spoken? When a prophet speaks in the name of the Lord, if the thing follow not, nor come to pass, that is the thing which the Lord hath not spoken, but the prophet has spoken presumptuously: therefore, thou shalt not be afraid of him" (Deuteronomy 18:21-22).

"For Jesus himself testified, that a prophet hath no honor in his own country" (John 4:44).

"Behold, I have told you before!" (Matthew 24:25).

Purpose: For the Work of the Ministry
Written on April 28, 1995
Ephesians 4:11-13, "to prepare the saints"
In response to America's memorial service for the Oklahoma bombing tragedy.

AN ANSWER TO THE TEARS... MY AMERICA!

I have heard the cry of my countrymen. I have seen the tears of the daughters of thine nation. And now do we lift up our voices in anxious prayer! Now do we seek His refuge and search Him out! And He has heard our cry, but He returned unto me a question. For the Lord do ask, "What is it that we require?" And we do answer for ourselves. We shall overcome! Singing "God Bless America" as if He is ours and ours alone. But do we examine ourselves that we might wonder? I think not! Indeed, our hearts act above reproach. And even our courts are in disarray, believing our rights to be above His laws.

He asks, are we the better for it? Oh, what a wretched nation we have become! Even our adversaries are beginning to know justice better than we do. And they are now set to look upon our calamity. Oh, America! For our democracy has blinded us, and we have back-slidden in our freedom! And the Lord do ask me, His servant among servants, how much freedom shall we require with our democracy? Shall your purpose be for an occasion to sin? But because His grace is so abundant, we are certain to misappropriate it in our freedom for He is mindful of our policies on Capitol Hill, and our amendments from place to place are indeed contrary to Him. Indeed, we are in opposition to His very Laws. But He is God, and He states, "I change not!" Is it not peculiar that the name of him whom the Lord has Christened is silenced even within our institutions of learning? And even now we begin to suffer loss not just in the heartland of our nation but from coast to coast. Listen up, for even the beauty of America has become tarnished! The Lord has rained a cleansing, but we are refusing a refreshing. I assure you we have not met His wrath, but by His chastening, we will learn from the absence of His Grace. For the elements of the earth shall consume us in our disobedience.

Think, oh Man. The Lord requires you to hear! Why, oh Gentiles, can't you rejoice in the salvation of Israel? Have ye not profited from their fall as an object lesson? Is not the very works of His hand made known to us through Israel? And now it is before us night and day for an understanding and as evidence. But knowledge we have refused, and wisdom we do cast out! Oh, but the Lord has placed a hot word upon my lips. He has lit a fire within my heart!

Requiring a proclamation, He says, Oh man… Loose the cause of Israel before their faces even before the earth. And make known the purpose of the Lord before the congregation. Establish the God of Israel for a demonstration of His power and His glory! For He is set once again to restore the Tabernacle of David before their eyes. And the Lord knows that you shall be jealous in His sight, ye Gentiles. For our concerns will be in opposition to His Agenda, which shall be *by the Word*. Let us turn our attention to Truth that we might see His Justice set against the nations who are contrary to His nation and His Son. For is this not but the very display of His mercy to those nations throughout the ages?

For we are in attendance in the Court of our God and know our sins. Therefore, the Lord has proved our guilt through the innocence of His Son! I say make way, for justice shall be served to the transgressors against Truth and Promise. Harden not your hearts against the knowing of His Ways. For it is a truth that the Lord has caused me to speak. May the people of God hear these words for this is the conclusion of the matter. For the Lord has a concern above our own… . America! How many of you remember that we serve the God of Israel? Can we bear it that we might gain from it? I pray the saints do accept it in humility. To promote Me or to protect yourselves, which gospel do we serve the Lord asks?

Church, I appeal to you to hear this line of thought, which do come by the Spirit. As Satan blinded Israel through their selfishness, and so they did stumble. Is he blinding even the saints that they might stumble over the Word concerning Israel? I affirm that our indifference has become equivalent to Israel's. Was not the Word written concerning Jesus and Israel refused to believe in that hour? Now the Word is written concerning Israel's return, and we do not consider it in our hour!

As Israel rejected the Christ in their ignorance, I have been made to see also that the Church Institution is in unbelief concerning the Hope of Israel's salvation. Oh, the wisdom of the Lord in the performing of His Test. What goes around has indeed come around! And I cannot refuse it or argue its point. This is righteousness at its finest, and I know God is the preparer of it. Church of Gentiles, be careful of having your own righteousness. Be careful indeed, for God is not subordinate to your thoughts nor your traditions but require our obedience to His thoughts… lest we fail also.

Therefore, do not dismay but prepare for instruction. The Lord has set before Him a new voice and given unto those a vision. And I do see an ancient promise set to be fulfilled, and it is a revelation. For the Lord did state, "I will pour out my Spirit and they shall prophesy of it." For indeed the time has come for the *Anointed One*. Remember, is not the time an appointed end to this world that another might come? I forewarn that you do not forget the Lord's covenant with Israel or shall you refuse to remember it being wise in your own conceit! It can be counted against you in the day the Lord should require you to believe it.

Therefore, this is my answer to your tears, oh America. As you choose to cast My Son from your democracy that other religions may abide. As you choose to make acceptable before Me man with man and woman with woman! As your politics approves gambling and your credit approves debt. So shall I permit it that you may fall from the weight of thy greed in your freedom. For it shall be a curse to you, and I shall sit back, and your cries I shall not hear. For then the Lord you shall be without, and in your diversity there will be calamity.

But to my Church, remember the Lord's decree of faith. Remember the prophecy that must yet be fulfilled by the Word for it is a more sure word. Remember thy First Love and His Kingdom that is to Come. Remember the judgment, which must be served through the revelation of My Son. Remember My Promise to Israel, for I will covet them in that hour. Are not all these things written in the same

Book for remembrance? Reality is about to check in upon the earth, and there is no excuse for not seeing that which can be seen and read and understood for the glory of God and His Truth. I pray thee judge not according to appearance but judge righteous judgment. Let us not say no to His Word for it is the Name of Jesus. And is it already written? Prepare my saints to wear Robes of Righteousness for there is a wedding to attend. Rejoice now. I say rejoice evermore in this truth. For by the grace of God do I bring you a minority report as did Joshua and Caleb. And how few did follow them for there was not one! Christ is before us; let us Hear Him for He states, "Behold, I have told you before."

But who shall love Truth that they might desire Righteousness be served? Our God has been merciful and full of patience that we should know His grace indeed. I commission your prayers for a prophet of the Lord has no honor… yet! And who shall believe such a report in the time that it should be known? But the righteousness of the Lord is my strength, and He shall be my shield. For the Lord loves the righteous one. So be ye righteous by wisdom, my Church. Wisdom does cry out into the streets and whispers gently before the saints. Where is righteousness that it might be performed? I thank God that His Word has been placed before us to know Him. For the Word states, "Through knowledge are the righteous delivered." Let us speak with unspeakable joy that a real Kingdom draws near for a silent thunder is set to roar, and the earth will be shakened!

In closing I say open thine heart to the seeing of His ways, and thou shalt be with Jesus for it is good that the Bride should know the coming of her Groom. That the wedding might be pure and holy… Come, the Lord do say. Come indeed! Even if need be repent that ye may come before Him. Come one and come all and be ye forgiven. AMEN AND AMEN.

FOURTH LETTER

Purpose: For the Perfecting of the Saints

Ephesians 4:11-13

"IN ALL FAIRNESS" SUCH IS THE LORD'S RIGHTEOUSNESS

Hear, Earth and all its inhabitants, the Word of the Lord for the time has come, and the moment has already been declared. But the people go about their way, unaware and so unconcerned, consumed in the serving of themselves, for themselves, night and day. They continuously gather only to be found without what they really need. Be still, those who are quick upon the earth, that you might hear. Be observant that you might see and come to know. For the time of the Lord's visitation draws near indeed. Now that the earth is full of the abundance of men and their inventions, what shall man conquer next that he can overcome by his own strength? By our intellect we have stood upon the moon and searched the very heavens for our comparison and have found none!

But that does not mean that there are none to be considered. For the Word of God sits upon our shelves that we might *hear* . . . *Thus saith the Lord!* But man rejects the God that is for the god he wants, much to his own hurt. Yeah, but the Word of God has withstood Time itself and has overcome the unbelief of those who choose unbelief. It has endured and continuously persevered throughout the ages, penned by His servants of the ancient days. Is not the Word even before you and I? Indeed, even the Word has overcome the judgment of the Tower of Babel. It has risen even above His stumbling nation to show the Lord stumbles not! Though I have scattered those at the Tower of Babel, did I not also bring man back together at Pentecost? How marvelous is the Lord! Has not the Lord translated His Word that the many tongues might receive it? For in this generation, who can not have it before him? Which one of us can give a worthy excuse of ignorance before the God of Israel? For the Spirit has published His Word and set forth His Works. Promoting it to the ends of the earth as the Lord said must be done… First!

And so has He performed it, for indeed no weapon has prospered against Him. Now can all the earth make a decision, yes, even a firm rejection? And can the whole earth not do it universally… collectively… and conclusively? For this is the wisdom of the Lord and the patience of His grace. That He waits! And has not our God also waited for man but to no avail! So many of us have gone astray and now even refuse to turn from sin. We have an excuse for every wrong and a blame for every fault. But where is our own account, and can it be hidden from God?

There is a thorn that God Himself has placed in the midst of the earth. And that old devil called Satan fights against the Word of God by blinding the world to His Word, and oh, what a multitude He has. For what ought to be a rose before the church has the appearance of a thorn to the earth. And the church is also ready to see it as a thorn except those who walk by the Word. And the Word is by the Spirit, and the Holy Spirit giveth us the wisdom of Christ. And His wisdom dictates a thorny issue, which shall determine true faith. That thorn is Israel, which shall be His rod of tension in the midst, a great time of decision for the whole world that they might believe in Jesus. It shall cause a trembling among the nations who have not His Word in the presence of their people nor His Hope in the depths of their hearts.

Am I not a God who can choose and yet deny, give grace and yet perform a test? Who can announce in ancient times things that are to be in the end times? Oh man, look and give reverence unto the Lord. What a merciful God we serve. For Israel shall be His sign upon the earth. A sign that shall be refused and is refused because the

Lord shall be refused. But He is the Holy God who owns justice and is entitle to perform it against all who walk in unbelief. For we serve a crucified savior who owns the right of retribution... Oh Earth! Take heed and study for I do require of My people that they might know Me.

How does the Lord try the nations like Israel the nation was tried? Why should Israel be the only nation to be measured against His Law and Truth? Listen up, ye nations, for the Lord is also set to try you as He did Israel! All ye Gentiles of the many nations, the Lord stands before us all by the Word through the rebirth of His nation as Christ stood before them in His Birth. So Christ fulfilled the scriptures literally that the reality of God might be known to us! At whose expense, Church? Whose stumbling caused you to be lifted up? Whose ignorance of the Lord was made public that the Gentiles would profit from? It is the power of God under demonstration through His nation that gave us His Truth. Giving us our salvation and our redemption and our hope even to be resurrected! Oh, He has given a stunning revelation for the time of the end and I do fall upon my face! Praise God from whom all knowledge flows that we might have wisdom from.

We ought to love Israel for the burden they were made to bear for we have gained! I forewarn you of this with deep mourning. Israel is the Root, and we are branches. We cannot separate ourselves from this truth or surely we shall stumble also! Oh Israel, cry out to the crucified One that He might prove His resurrection, and by your repentance surely He must come for His Word promises *it* to us all. And now Israel is fulfilling the Word unawares. To make known the reality of who God is before those who choose to deny the Cross of Jesus and the redemption of Israel. I have found that angel of light who deceiveth the whole world. Church, none of our goodness shall prevail against the deceiver of this kind. But Truth and only Truth will Stand that God Himself may be glorified in righteousness. Will the real Israel please stand up! Is the church Israel or is Israel... Israel? Cannot God have two vessels of His making, or will man deny God the privilege only to lose due to his own selfishness? This I forewarn to all.

Satan whispers, "Did God really say He would restore Israel?" I proclaim emphatically by the Word that it states Yes... Yes... and Yes! God is indeed standing the Nation up, and the world refuses to believe. And even the churches contend with God and consider it not. Therefore, whose side are we really on, Church? The Word or the World? Shall it be what we think, or shall it be what actually can be seen and yet we refuse? Yes, what a mighty God we serve. For the Word does state: "Let every man be a liar that God may be true" and it will be so in the hour that He demonstrates it.

I am commanded to write the vision and Stand in the gap as a Cry in the wilderness. For the Battle is set in the Valley of Jehoshaphat, and Jerusalem is God's place of visit! He will not be denied in that final Hour. For it will be His moment in Time. God's thoughts indeed are higher than our thoughts, as high as the heavens above earth. Fear the Lord God and judge not, for the law of man is no better than the heart of the man. But the Law of God brings long life to those who follow it. And the Law of Christ even saves the soul for eternal blessings! So hear this as I close.

Ask God the question that He awaits... Why is Israel back? Let the Church pray this before the throne of God. And I heard His answer in the depths of my spirit as it was declared. Thus, saith the Lord by the Spirit of Truth. Righteousness means 'In All Fairness.' Can I the Lord stand before one nation only and require they know Me and not also require from all other nations that they know Me as well by Test? In all fairness, Israel had to believe in Christ's First Coming. Would it be right not to try the Gentiles' belief in His Second Coming? Read the Book to See!

In all fairness, people of the earth, don't you want equal opportunity also? So shall it be that the nations shall have its trial as Israel did. That Righteousness might be performed and Justice can be served to those who make the same error and have even a lesser excuse than Israel for they are an example. Remember, except when our righteousness exceeds the righteousness of the Pharisee, we will not see any better than they did. Let the black man see only black and the white man see only white. And every kind shall see it their way! For every man shall take hold of his tradition at the expense of losing Christ. The Lord states, "For My Word is not in you that you might believe in Me only." As the Jew, so shall be the Gentile. The Lord God does try the heart!

I prophesy to you this as Jesus was nailed to the cross, so is Israel to be nailed by a world of unbelief. And this time the Lord Himself shall answer Israel's cry, and the True God shall be made Known. To dust shall all the religions of this world crumble, even the denominations! But not the Word and neither the believer that overcomes by faith in Jesus name.

This is the Work of our Gospel in this generation. Be ye not afraid! This is the Seal which the Lord has graced me to open and to see by His Word. This is the Prophecy that now must come, and God Himself shall no more be seen darkly through obscure glass but as clear as crystal in pure righteousness. And the prophecy of the Seventieth Week of Daniel will sum up all things as written. For the Woman and her Man Child is Israel and the Lord Jesus. And the rejected Son will yet be received by the Nation to the Glory of God. As Savior to the Gentiles, let the Lord demonstrate also Messiah to the Jews! Let all men take their places and declare before God where ye stand. For the Deliverance has Come that the world will know what a mighty God we serve!

I AM AFTER THEE, OH LORD

My Lord and My God
Hear my cry and know my praise… For I am after thee.
For I have searched the low places…
Yea, the hidden places have I sought thee out.
In my soul do I climb to the peak of the highest mountain
That I may Find the God of my salvation
Am I not lifted up by thy Grace
And made to sing by thine abundant mercies?
I am after thee, Oh Lord.
And in my flesh I cannot find thee.
But only in my spirit shall you be found.
I travel the path of the bumblebee, seeking thee,
Seeming to have no direct path…
Yet only is my destination made sure by your leading hand.
And so I am found by thee, and my path do become straight.
I am made a servant of the Lord
And a friend unto Jesus, the Rock of my salvation.
By thy Spirit am I broken, but by thy Spirit
Was I strengthened. Think well of me, Oh Lord,
That I might not be made to battle the Wind of the Spirit
For I do seek to rest as thou giveth Man in his beginning.
In me there is a secret storm calmed only by a still, small voice.
Yes, even a silent thunder
For my Lord will know the praise that dwells in me.
For it is a certainty that I shall not be silenced.
And let not even sin encroach upon me
For will not my spirit hide from thee.
Thou I may stumble, the power of thy
salvation will be holding me up.
And I shall forever repent for only thee is forever righteous.
Only thee is forever without sin, my Lord Jesus.
Therefore, I rest my case under Thy cross
And seek no more for my peace… It is found!
For it is thy Spirit that has determined that it should be found.

Thou has heard my cry, and my voice has been heard.
Therefore, thou shall forever hear my praise
For thy sacrifice has cleansed me
And thou salvation has made me whole.
I am after thee, Oh Lord, for thou is a secret God,
And you search for seekers after you and you only.
Blessed are those who are after the Lord
And look for Him daily in the way of goings… Amen.

THE OTHER SIDE OF THE CROSS

There's something amiss when the creation resists
all that the Creator stands for.
As I gaze at the cross, it reflects a world lost
With Christ knocking on every Door.
Man thinking himself good, did that which he thought he should.
With charges of blasphemy and plenty of religiosity.
Refused to believe the Word… being filled with animosity.
Delivering the Lord to the Court of courts.
And so the trial did promptly begin.
He was alone, having not a character witness, nor even a friend
And when the judge could find no law against him,
Washing his hands, I'm sure he did what he can.
All except free this sinless man.
Crucify… crucify was the outcry from the crowd!
And the Law that was became no Law at all, and yet God smiled!
So there our Savior laid with outstretched arms,
Demonstrating His love despite the harm.
And while every man is born in sin,
The injustice we profess doesn't compare
to the injustice He was placed in.
There's something amiss when the creation resists
All that the Creator stands for even now like then.
But an empty Tomb was God's reward for a work well done.
Not to be hid, the Lord shone forth His only Son.
For Jesus showed His love toward all mankind.
And now there is life after death in only His name you will find!
But let the other side of the cross speak also.
That what and who we are has surely been exposed.
For in God's love so openly displayed
We did show our wretchedness that day.
And God's Law of Love soundly defeated
Our law of justice, which we misdeeded.
Our anger truly showed only to see the peace of God flow.
Our fearfulness for no reason illuminated God's love for all seasons.

The Cross is the meeting place for all of this.
And believe it or not, the Creator let the creation insist!
So let us remember the wisdom the Cross is meant to bring.
God will have His day of justice that righteousness,
which is fairness ought ring.
For the other side of the cross speaks well of His return.
Sitting on the right-hand side of the Father, this He earned!
But there are yet those who choose not to believe
Like doubting Thomas, they say "Not by
faith but by sight must I see!"
But blessed are those who believe and have not seen!
For no more is God a mystery neither is He a dream.
You see, Grace and Mercy have been born out of Injustice.
And it is the other side of the cross that gives us this message.
That our way of justice means nothing
when Truth demands His Return.
For this is why the Word declares the Earth shall Burn
And we who are caught up in His Rapture shall bear witness.
Revealing that the Other Side of the Cross
was a lesson that went Unlearned!

LET THERE BE

In the midst of Change… Let there be Stillness.
In the midst of Disappointment… Let there be Contentment.
In the midst of Confusion… May there be Patience.
Yes! In the Hour of our Testing… Always let there be Faith!
And in our moment of Despair… Let there yet be Hope.
Despite being in the midst of these Calamities,
Remember that Jesus Christ can indeed Cope!
Let there be Silence… That we might whisper our Prayers.
Let there be Joy… That we might sing our Songs.
And let there be Peace That we should wait on the Lord however Long.
Finally, if there is one thing that we must let there be,
Let there be Love and that it might be among us All.
For without such in our hearts might we Fall.
So as we grow, we may yet shed a few more Tears.
Seeking a more perfect Kingdom.
Nevertheless, let us come Near.
Therefore, I pray for the Spirit of Harmony.
May all these things be found in you.
And that a Healing may begin within us each.
For a testimony of what Christ's Love can do.
Let these things be not without me,
And most assuredly, let these things be not without you!

CLOSING THOUGHTS:
A BACK-TO-BASIC GOSPEL

I HOPE YOU ENJOYED the reading of this collection of inspired writings. To me it was an experience to be revealed even though such a "telling" was not my initial purpose or desire. I declare that God moved me in a way that He must be spoken of, and so I ultimately have done just that. It is indeed bold to declare oneself a prophet, and I do not mean to offend anyone with this title, but I do believe God is restoring this ministry in preparation of Christ's return… The true prophet will do as the scripture requires in 1 Corinthians 14:3: "But he that prophesieth speaketh unto men to edify, exhort and to comfort." I hope this material produces the fruit of faith and joy.

In the article titled "And the Hand of the Lord Was Upon Me," I make reference of another series of articles not a part of these collective works. This effort titled "Seven Letters Detailing the Prophetic Framework of the Return of Christ" was written before any article in this book and gives a detailed account of prophetic events that are stated in scripture and is also proclaimed to be revealed in an *inspired* setting. The four letters of prophetic utterances represent a condensed version of the Seven Letters, which have common names such as letters but are very different in style, format, and approach. The *Seven Letters* exercises the gift of prophecy written in a more formal and conventional manner. It has the supporting scripture and fully grasp the complexities and paradoxes that can exist when studying biblical prophecy. It is recommended reading to the Institution of Christianity regardless of denominational setting or national/racial heritage and can be found on www.authorhouse.com. website.

I have shared these writings with individuals many times and seen how people have been blessed by them. All I desire is for people to see what I see. These writings hopefully should educate as well as forewarn because there is a refreshing to the Gospel coming that will shake all our comfort zones. Christ will be the center-piece as always, but according to the Word, Israel is His purpose for returning, and we must be prepared to say Amen and Amen! Salvation will be Israel's at last, and my hope is we don't reject this Truth coming as written in the Word as Israel rejected his First coming, which was in the Word. Sad to say, despite the forewarnings, wisdom dictates many will reject this reality to their own hurt for it is already written.

Satan is revealing his mastery of making Man not see what he should be able to see. So it was in the Garden of Eden. So it was two thousand years ago when Israel failed and put Christ on the Cross, and so it is even now as the Gentile world, including unborn again, unaware, unbelieving church folk, is being led to put Israel on the Cross. Could God be testing us in much the same way as Israel was tested? And are we and even the churches above being tested? I certainly think not! Oh, the wisdom of the Lord! Hindu, Buddhism, Islam, Atheism, witchcraft, and every other false religion is about to be cast down. This is why the Battle of Armageddon is on the borders of Israel. As God is set to demonstrate one thing and one thing only, and that is… *What Truth Is and Where it Sits!* Now it comes down to *he that overcome and not a denominational preference but a realization of His Word and that it is Heard!*

If you notice, this is not religion but belief in His Word by a born-again experience with a personal relationship with Christ. Far more than just church, a distinction that needs to be acknowledged more and more with each passing day. May this book help that process to begin encouraging you to look at God's Word with a fresh anointing. Bless to see the future according to God's perspective. My heart cries out constantly for the world to hear these things, but they are so consumed. But every now and then, God sends me someone who does *hear*, and that makes this effort worth every bit of my time. And so I press on with this New Gospel, which is bridging Israel and the Church into one holy entity in preparation of the Kingdom to Come, led by Christ "Lord of Lord and King of Kings." Such is a Back-to-Basic Gospel!

AND THEN CAME
THE RAPTURE...

When I began my prophetic studies, I did not even know anything about the event known as the Rapture. It was never a topic of discussion in Sunday school classes or sermon preaching. It was after much biblical study that I begin reading from Christian schools of thought and writers such as, Hal Lindsey, Tim Lahaye and others that such an event became of interest. My earlier works don't dialogue on the subject, though it is ironic how I felt the Christians were absent from the tribulation period. I am not here to debate whether it's a pre, mid or post. I am here to state my position and why.

I can now say, that the Rapture "caught up" is an official biblical doctrine found in 1 Thessalonians 4: 13-18. Introduced by apostle Paul as inspired by the Holy Spirit and addressed to the community of churches for that great day of the Lord. It reads "But I do not want you to be ignorant, brethren concerning those who have fallen asleep, lest you sorrow as others who have no hope. For if we believe that Jesus has died and rose again, even so God will bring with Him those who sleep in Jesus. For this we say to you by the word of the Lord, that we who are alive and remain until the coming of the Lord will by no means precede those who are asleep. For the Lord Himself will descend from heaven with a shout, with the voice of an archangel, and with the trumpet of God. And the dead in Christ shall rise first. Then we who are alive and remain shall be caught up together with them in the clouds to meet the Lord in the air. And thus, we shall always be with the Lord. Therefore, comfort one another with these words." The doctrine is quite specific wit details and even double emphasis.

We are instructed by Paul not to be unaware of this doctrine of hope which is also for comfort. And yet there is silence among the bulk of churches. The ministry of this event as supernatural as it is, is debated more often about when than if. I am sensing something when I continue to read chapter five of 1 Thessalonians right after the doctrine is given. In 5:1-3 Paul declares "When they say peace and safety, then sudden destruction" scholars have called this the false peace and I can agree with that. However, I sense more than just that. This could also be an indication of the signing of the 70th Week of Daniel also known as 7-year Tribulation period. This supports a false peace. The signing event of the covenant could generate jubilation and such an applause to the world but due to its Terms & Conditions be offensive to God. Is this why God advises Christians to be sober and not sleeping as stated in the chapter? It is written in this same chapter in verse 9 "For God did not appoint us to wrath but to obtain salvation through our Lord." No time or day is given but I do believe a sign is. It also appears the church is here at the very beginning of the tribulation period in order to see this event. This means we are caught up after the signing and not before it. The timing is still imminent and no man knows the day but it does prepare our hearts for the blessed hope and earnest expectation for the saints that it should be in our prayers as we align our thoughts to God's purpose and to be where Jesus is. No doubt about achieving peace being a good thing but will it be at the expense some biblical deviation about Israel and or the Church central doctrine given by God? This is why I am a pretribber with confidence and it's fully backed by scripture. Perhaps, the closer we get the better we can see. The sheer power of the Word is that the word is before us to be studied. Be watchful and pray as the Lord comes for the Bride.

IF YOU SHOULD HAVE FURTHER INTEREST IN HOW
THE SPIRIT HAS MOVED ME TO WRITE, PLEASE GO TO
authorhouse.com FOR MY PUBLISHED WORK TITLED
SEVEN LETTERS
DETAILING THE PROPHETIC FRAMEWORK OF
THE RETURN OF CHRIST
AGAIN, I PERSONALLY THANK YOU FOR YOUR
TIME AND DESIRE ABOVE ALL THAT YOU GO TO
THE PRAYER ROOM IN YOUR CLOSET THAT YOU
SHOULD HEAR THE VOICE OF HIS SPIRIT. FOR IT
IS WRITTEN UNTO JEREMIAH 33:3: *"CALL UNTO ME
AND I WILL ANSWER AND SHOW THEE GREAT AND
MIGHTY THINGS WHICH THOU KNOWEST NOT."*
Such is the duty of us as Christians.
Let us not be deceived, for what should be obvious to us.
Obviously is not! Such is the work of the adversary.
He doesn't even want you to think Christ is coming back.
But I say come, Lord, do come!

9 7 9 8 8 9 6 7 2 3 0 1 1